Dragons, Caterpillars, Frogs and Toads

Read Aloud Now.

The Power of Words will Transform Your Child's Life.

It is never too late, start reading now and may you be filled with joy!

Susan M. Jarvis

Susan M. Jarvis

Cover design and illustration by Shari Fisher

First Published by Platypus Publishing 2023

Dragons, Caterpillars, Frogs and Toads

PLATYPUS

PUBLISHING

Susan M. Jarvis

Dragons, Caterpillars, Frogs and Toads

Give your children the gift of imagination, give them dragons, pink, white, green. Give them wings, outer-space, caves and tunnels and everything in between.

Give your children the gift of transformation, like a very, hungry caterpillar to a beautiful butterfly, use a story and a lullaby.

Give your children the gift of wisdom from the friendship of an imaginary frog and toad, do it through books, milk and home-made cookies with a chocolate chip.

CONTENTS

Introduction   5

Dragons and Why Reading Matters and Why Just Reading is Not
Enough   9

Everything, Everywhere What to Read Aloud   23

What is the Best Time and Place to Read?   29

Show Up Take Action   35

How to Interact with a Book   38

Not all Kids are the Same   55

Adaptive Equipment   62

Affirmations   64

Frequently Asked Questions   69

What Not to Do   72

Book List   74

Resources   88

Certainty   92

Acknowledgments   94

About the Author   95

Introduction

❧

"We have everything to gain and
no time to waste."
Meghan Cox Gurdon

We all want our children to be healthy, happy and safe. And we want so much more. But wanting for something without action is not enough.

There is a surefire way for you the parent to be active in your child's future success. By reading every day to your child, talking to your child about what you read, listening to your child, asking each other questions, connecting, laughing and loving you are creating an open door to a happy, confident, caring life for your child.

The rewards of daily reading aloud to your child may not be evident immediately so be patient because there really is a pot of gold at the end of this rainbow.

As a teenage Mom, I knew next to nothing about raising a child. Although, I read to my daughter, the impact and importance of reading, the importance of interacting with the book and the importance of opening up her world and her imagination were yet to be discovered. But what I have learned as a parent, a Speech and Language Pathologist for over 30 years and a volunteer in Neonatal Intensive Care Units are many lessons I can share with you.

The world we live in right now is a place of uncertainty about our climate, the safety of our water, air and food, fears that come with an epidemic, the cost and availability of gas, food and housing, shootings and violence. Our children are not immune to knowing these struggles. Much of this feels like it is outside of our control. However, parents have the potential, by reading aloud daily, to bring feelings of safety, hope and love while simultaneously building new pathways in their child's brain, that give them skills that will take them forward in life.

As I promote the importance of daily reading there is a rapidly growing, unprecedented surge in efforts to ban books. According to PEN, an organization dedicated to preserving and celebrating free expression, fifty advocacy groups pushed to ban books during the last school year. These groups according to the New York Times (December,13, 2022), "have grown vastly more organized, interconnected, well-funded - and effective." One individual, who caused books to be banned in a Florida school district, supposedly did not even read the books nor did that individual have a student enrolled in that school district.

Book bans are not the only problem. The Department of Justice states, "The link between academic failure and delinquency, violence, and crime is tied to reading failure. Over 70% of inmates in America's prisons cannot read above a fourth-grade level." There is a better way.

I have written this book, because of my personal love of books, the ongoing social problems, and my passion for children's rights including children's speech and language development. This book is a clear and concise description of the importance of reading aloud for your child's future success. This book gives ideas on what to read, when to read, and how to read so your child has fun and experiences precious moments that affect his or her future. There is a section for parents of infants who may be hospitalized in the Neonatal Intensive Care Unit, and a section for parents of children with special needs. Frequently asked questions are included, along with suggestions on what not to do. Examples of specific ways to build upon the experience of reading the book from observation of the cover illustration to rhyming and sound development to questions for thoughtful conversations are also explored.

This book will save you time and energy, and guide you along the way. Read the list of spectacular books, answers to frequently asked questions, the list of affirmations for building confidence, and the list of resources such as how to access free books from Dolly Parton's Imagination Library.

Reading aloud is not a magic pill, but it will give your children a foundation to cope with problems. They will have speech, vocabulary and thinking skills to express their thoughts and feelings and build self-confidence. Waiting for kindergarten puts your child significantly behind the children who have had stories read to them daily. Roxanne J. Coady, so clearly states, "Books can change lives, yes, and so can the lack of them."

Surround your child with books.

Dragons
and Why Reading Matters
and Why Just Reading is Not Enough

> "When I say to a parent, "read
> to your child," I don't want it to
> sound like medicine. I want it to
> sound like chocolate."
> ***Mem Fox***

There is a surefire path that will open your child to new worlds, stimulate brain development, build vocabulary and speech, increase memory and focus and so much more. And it is outright fun.

As parents, you get to build lives filled with dreams, beauty, goodness, determination, optimism, gratitude, compassion, love and joy. You can replace fear with hope for a fulfilling life for you, your child and your whole family.

This book will help you navigate the future.

Maybe your infant arrived early, too early to come home and your baby is staying in the hospital. Maybe your child was born with an unexpected disability. You feel lost, confused and concerned for the future. Maybe you question your confidence and ability to raise a child.

My intent is to empower you and your children. This journey of yours will be easy, entertaining, practical and magical.

The answer is Reading. Reading aloud to your child every day and interacting through asking questions, talking, listening and loving is the number one, most powerful, impactful activity that will shape your child's future success. The life sustaining necessities of love, food, clothing, housing and safety of course come first. Reading aloud and interacting with your child is simple, easy and fun, and a great bedtime ritual for sleepy parents and children.

You do not need a college degree or a high school diploma or any special credentials. What you do need is a book, a little time and a heart full of love. You cannot fail. If you are a teenage mom, parents of adopted children, single parent, grandparent, or parent of a child with special needs, reading to your child is the number one most impactful activity for your child's future success.

Children, whose parents read them five books a day, start kindergarten having heard about 1.4 million more words than children who were not read to, according to a study from Ohio State University in 2019. This is now being called "The million-word gap".

Children, whose parents read them just one book a day, will hear about 290,000 more words by kindergarten. Children who are brought up listening to stories are being set up for school success. All these words, this expanding vocabulary, equates to better skills in listening and speaking. When a child has more words, they are better at communicating. They are also better at understanding the communication of others.

This richer vocabulary also means greater world knowledge. Richer vocabulary predicts greater income and success in adulthood including an increased likelihood of attending college and owning their own homes. This success starts with parents reading aloud to their children.

The first year of your baby's life is an amazing, optimal time for your baby's brain development. Brain development between birth and age 1 is greater than any other time. Not reading aloud to your baby is a missed opportunity. You can start reading aloud to your child, whether your child is one, two, three, four or five years of age. 90% of a child's brain is developed by age five. Football players do not suit up for the game after the game is over. In other words, game day starts now. Make the choice to read aloud to your kids every day.

The benefits of reading aloud to your children include building skills related to:

- Attention
- Memory
- Listening
- New words
- Variety of words
- Rhyming
- Grammar
- Problem solving
- Social skills
- World knowledge
- Cognition
- Imagination
- Parent-child bonding
- Speech development
- Calming oneself

Attention

Even a toddler, on the floor holding a block, can have attention to both what you are reading and on the block they are holding. When you ask a question or say, "Look at the fox," the child will focus on your voice and look on the page at the fox. Children are open to bringing their attention to all the stimuli in their environment, but your voice is special. Your voice is more significant and important. Make it soft or loud, silly or serious to accompany the meaning and feeling of what you are reading.

Memory

There are many kinds of memory. Memory for numbers include things like your salary or telephone numbers. Memory includes recent events or memory for the past, memories of your childhood, or the color of your first car. When you are chatting with a friend on the phone, you might say, "Remember when I told you about what happened at the cafe on 6th Street?"

When you speak with your child use different memory strategies. Listening to stories, especially the same story, read repeatedly builds the memory skills in your child's brain long before they have the speech skills to express what it is about. We all need excellent memory skills to build a foundation for our lives.

Our memories help us make associations to build a framework of understanding. Here is an example. You take a trip to visit Grandma, and Grandma has a dog. You read Old MacDonald Had a Farm and there is a dog on the farm. Then you read Where's Spot? And then Clifford the Big Red Dog. With each new experience, the child's understanding of "dog" grows from the one at Grandma's house, to the farm, to little dogs, big dogs, and so forth. Remembering the word "dog" and having new experiences with the word "dog" builds associations. By reading to your child, you have made their world bigger.

Listening

Listening to stories builds focus naturally. When you switch roles and your child tells you the story (before they can read) you will watch how they turn the pages, follow a sequence, and look for what they remember. What did they hear? How many times do we listen yet miss the details? You might get the main idea but were you listening to the details? Children are novices at learning to do it all.

There is a question on a language and listening test designed for grade school children that asks "What is the color of the small, grey pony?" Do you know how many children say, the pony is pink ? Do you think they were listening?

Re-reading a story allows the child's brain to listen again to the story and gain more information. Read their favorite books over and over. They are learning more each time.

New Words and a Variety of Words

Written language expresses thoughts with words heard less frequently in conversation.Word combinations like sandy shore, dark woods, humming insect are not common in everyday vocabulary. This is why children hearing the word combination "monkeys jumping on the bed" from a storybook is so delightful. It is unusual, unexpected and not found in conversational speech. I have never once eaten my cereal and discussed how monkeys were jumping on my bed. Written language read aloud is rich and delicious. In the story, The Little Engine That Could, children hear descriptive word combinations "rumbled over the tracks", "plate glass window", "passenger engine" and "indignantly" that add color, sound and texture to the story.

Children who listen to stories will be familiar with so many more words and ideas. A familiar word like "run" used in a new way is something to point out in the stories you read. Runny noses, the refrigerator that stops running, run a fever, the water left running, she was running for President or he hit a home run are examples of how we use the word run in such a variety of ways. Words are so much fun to explore. Not reading will put your child at a disadvantage.

Through the stories you read and the world of imagination you can bring your child anywhere: the farm, the city, a mountain, river, a Space Center, foreign nation or another state. With each new place you find in the story, there is a variety of new word knowledge to be gained.

Rhyming

Rhyming brings little minds the understanding that words are made of sounds, and just one sound changes the meaning of the word. Cat and hat sound alike at the end, but the beginning sound makes it a different word.

Rhyming helps the listener to become familiar with word families such as bit, hit, sit, fit, pit. When word families are recognized reading is easier. When speech language pathologists test for listening/auditory discrimination skills, the student is asked to compare similarities and differences between sounds. Which word does not rhyme cat, hat, ball, bat?

Dr. Seuss's books are masterpieces of the flow and fun of rhyming. The cat in the box would clearly never be as delightful as the Cat in the Hat.

Grammar

Grammar, the rules of American English, are taught in school through formal, structured lessons. A natural learning of the structure of language occurs through repeatedly hearing the word patterns in stories read aloud to children. They also learn through the conversations they hear every day. Children who have been read to will use the grammar they hear in these stories. More and more stories give them oodles of opportunities to hear word order, word combinations, adjectives, adverbs, idioms and more.

In my house, while growing up, if we used improper grammar, we had to stop and say it correctly right then and there. with?" Children learn words from parents, friends, television and of course stories. Learning grammar lays a foundation for understanding a common language. Learning grammar from stories read to us in natural and easy.

Problem solving

Children learn about problem solving through listening to stories. Stories start with a main character wanting something. Then, there is the problem of getting what they want. The story ends with the resolution. Winnie the Pooh wants honey. The Pigeon wants to stay up late. Frog and Toad are learning how to be friends. Through the stories, the characters fail and try again. The Big Bad Wolf tried to blow down three houses. After reading the story, ask your child what the characters wanted. The wolf was hungry and wanted to eat. The pigs wanted to be left alone. They did not want to be eaten. Ask your child what do we do when we are hungry? What do we do when we want to be left alone? There is not just one answer. In discussing the story, your child might have a new, unique way to help the character solve the problem. Find out. Did the characters solve their problems alone or did they get help? What does your child think about solving problems?

Social and Emotional Skills

Learning about manners, feelings, teamwork, responsibility, inclusivity and taking turns can all be found in stories. These skills are developed when adults interact with the story and the child. Who helped the Little Red Hen? What happened? Ask your child, "How did you feel when that happened in the story?" Ask the child why the character acted in a particular way? This teaches perspective. Was it funny or sad? Why?

When story characters are animals, usually with human characteristics, it opens the door for opportunities to notice that though outwardly different, inwardly we all have feelings and using animals to teach empathy is something children can relate to and can learn to see another's perspective.

Another way adults can interact with the story and the child is through having a conversation about the moral of the story. My last work assignment was at a school designed for children with physical disabilities and health impairments. The other speech pathologists and myself acted out a story for the students titled <u>Tacky the Penguin</u> about the importance of being true to yourself even if you are a little different. I played Tacky the penguin who was different. This story provided a fun, interactive experience with a powerful message.

World Knowledge

If you cannot travel even just a few miles from your home, books can take you around the globe, under the oceans, inside tunnels, through forests and to the landmarks in your own city. Some of my former students in Buffalo, New York had never seen Lake Erie or Niagara Falls, though it was only a short drive from where they lived. Bring your children knowledge of the world. Let them know there are children just like them, but those children enjoy different foods, speak different languages, and sing different songs. Yet, they might play the same games and sports and watch the same television shows.

Cognition and Imagination

Cognition is thinking, the process your brain goes through to acquire information and make sense of it.

Imagination is what happens as you listen to the story and form mental pictures. It is the writer's imagination that asked the questions to make the stories such as How much do you love me? What happens when you give a mouse a cookie?, What happened to the old lady who swallowed a fly?, Where's Spot?

It is the Illustrator's imagination that paints the pictures of what they see in their mind. It is you, the parent, who sparks and sharpens your child's brain and inspires the fantastic imaginations of your children through reading aloud to them.

Parent-Child Bonding

Reading aloud to your child is a beautiful time for bonding. Bonding is a biological and social-emotional need of all humans and absolutely essential for babies to thrive. Bonding occurs when you smile, feed, bathe, and cuddle your babies. Bonding occurs when you get on the floor and crawl around with your toddler, put them on your back and crawl some more. Bonding occurs when you hug, rock, giggle, play catch, sing, dance, and read aloud to your children.

Sharing the experience of stories, talking and listening, asking questions, is an exquisite way to spend time together every day to bond one-on-one or as a whole family.

Creating a bedtime ritual with snuggling and stories helps children feel safe and special. That special feeling of love and safety will be reflected back to you. You have nothing to lose in this journey and so very much to gain.

Speech Development

Children are born communicators! Their first spoken word may not arrive before age one but they have already cried, laughed, fussed, babbled and screamed. As you read to your child, their brains are busily decoding your words into meaningful units. They are learning the word orders we use. Mommy does not say, "Me love you." She says, "I love you."

Your baby watches your mouth and imitates vowels first and then m m m m m, b b b b b, p p p p. Those are the first sounds, and the more complex sounds like ch and th follow later on.

Reading aloud constructs the bridge from sounds alone to sounds that carry meaning, then to sounds representing the name of those things in the illustrations, then sounds used to name feelings, people, animals and colors.

A child learning the sounds of language, word order, rules, and the use of language and speech from listening to stories read aloud is magnificent.

Calming Oneself

Observing people on an airplane, a train or bus, you will see many of the passengers calmly reading. In preschool, students listen to a story before taking a nap. Waiting in line at the grocery store, customers page through a magazine calmly awaiting their turn. Reading is calming for babies, for children, for teenagers, for all of us. A benefit of reading aloud to your children includes the calming and soothing effect so important for their well-being.

The benefits of reading aloud daily to your child and interacting through the shared book experiences cannot be summed up sufficiently by this guide. So do it and see for yourself. Just a reminder...it is just as much about the journey as it is the result. Do it your way and enjoy the adventure.

Be yourself.

Relax.

Reading aloud is a simple, practical action to expand your child's world, stimulate their brains, and entertain them as well. Make it fun.

Now that you have the mindset of a powerful parent pursuing the path to a successful present and future for your child, let's get started.

Everything, Everywhere
What to Read Aloud

P rint is everywhere. Children under the age of five recognize the MacDonald's logo and the Disney logo. They also know Apple, the logo and the fruit. When interviewed, one five-year old knew the apple with a bite missing represented the Apple Store.

When my first child Bridget was little, she would shout out every "H" as we drove in the car. It was the white capital "H" inside the blue square symbolizing a hospital. We lived across the street from the hospital. Bridget seemed to love the letter "H". We were not using flashcards or teaching her, she was just exploring her world and it was fun.

My students and I would travel through the school locating all the EXIT signs. The students then began to recognize, with delight other signs including Pool, Nurse, Office and Speech Therapy.

Where are kids exposed to print?

- TV
- Stores
- Cereal boxes
- Diaper boxes
- EXIT signs
- Games
- Food labels; milk, juice, M&Ms
- Street signs; your street, STOP, Bike lane
- Elevator, up, down
- Holiday catalogues
- Doors; push, pull
- Airports
- Appliances; start, off
- And more

So where do you start?

Babies like colorful books with large pictures and few words. They like books they can sit on, put in their mouth, pull and tug. Board books are great for babies because they are so durable. Not all baby books are indestructible so save the more fragile books just for story time.

Your baby may not yet understand the words you are reading but they love to be held. They are listening to you speak and it is teaching them the sounds of language. Your scent and your voice are soothing. Babies need bonding and love in order to thrive. You are successfully meeting emotional needs and building communication skills by reading aloud to them.

Include Moms, Dads, older siblings, grandparents, and nannies in reading aloud times. It just adds more voices, more calming, more learning and more love.

Babies adore baby books. Baby does this, baby makes faces, baby does that. Try it and see for yourself.

If there is no book nearby, just read what you are reading. My youngest daughter would be swaddled in a blanket, so comfy in her Dad's lap, and he would read her the newspaper or a magazine. She was happy and I was recovering from surgery. All was well.

I keep two of my children's favorite baby books in a box in the closet. Hop Like a Bunny and Dance like a Bear; A Book About Things I Can Do written by Ed Cunningham and illustrated by Mary Hamilton is a board book we read over and over and over again. All the pages have fallen out. Yet, it remains adorable and readable. The book is so simple and filled with joy. It is not about things the child cannot do. It is a book about things they can do!

"I can bend way down and touch my toes.

Or pick up my socks.

And I can make things with my building blocks." Ed Cunningham

Why Do You Love Me? Written by Mabel Watts and illustrated by Katherine Sampson was the other favorite book I saved. This book has tape along the binding and more tape at the cover's edge. This book tells the story of Billy, a very small bear cub and his wild and wooly Mother. Billy misbehaves sometimes but his Mama loves him all the time.

Gertrude the Goose that Forgot by Joanna C. Galdone was another favorite story. It was a library book we borrowed countless times. Now, I wish we had purchased the book for it brings back precious memories.

Some older children's books are now being updated and reprinted. The Three Billy Goats Gruff comes in various renditions. I prefer the words in the Little Golden Book. The billy goats go trip trap, trip trap over the bridge. Then the Troll roars, "Who is that trip trapping over my bridge?" "It is I, Big Billy Goat Gruff."

The Three Billy Goats Gruff by Paul Galdone is illustrated with large, bold billy goats with large eyes and big horns. The troll is quite ugly and his image fills an entire page. Yet the text lacks the rhythmic quality of the other version.

Read both versions and see which one you like better and which one your child likes better. This is a baby book and it is a book that is appropriate for deeper conversations as your child grows up.

When deciding what to read, use the list in this book, ask friends for recommendations, go to the library, search the internet for lists of children's books, visit local bookstores, find books at Goodwill and other thrift stores, and attend school book fairs. Choose story books, picture books, chapter books, fiction and non-fiction. Pick themes such as animals, engineering, sports, space, cars, boats or dance. You name it, there are probably authors interested in that subject as well.

Get a library card for yourself and one for your child. The whole family can get library cards. My local library grants library cards to kids from birth on up. The first library book I ever borrowed as a child was Mike Mulligan and His Steam Shovel by Virginia Lee Burton. I can still see it sitting on the bottom shelf of the library. Using my library card for the first time made me feel so proud and grown up.

Dragons, Caterpillars, Frogs and Toads

Find your childhood favorite book. Read it to your child. Talk about why it was your favorite. Talk to the baby, the toddler or the five-year old.

What is the Best Time and Place to Read?

"There are many ways to enlarge
your child's world. Love of books
is the best of all."
Jackie Kennedy

S etting up a bedtime ritual of reading before your child goes to sleep more than any other time of day, unlocks the magic and mystery of reading aloud and creating a safe, loving, caring, nurturing experience. To create a ritual, it must be consistent. In other words, Read every night. Rituals provide structure. After the chaos of a busy day, the end of the day is predictable. This lessens a child's anxieties and fears.

A young boy living in a dangerous Boston neighborhood found solace in an empty deodorant bottle kept by the side of his bed. The label read "guaranteed 100% safe." Even babies experience anxiety. But a warm bottle or breast, swaddling, (wrapping the baby snuggly in a blanket) and a soft voice reading a story help bring relaxation and rest.

Most families have rituals such as Friday night pizza or Sunday morning pancakes, holidays with the relatives, or a weekly Zoom call with the grandparents. Even taking out the garbage is a ritual preformed weekly on the same day of the week, in the same place each time. It is necessary to turn off the TV and leave the phone in another room.

There will be days when you are exhausted. There is a pile of laundry, the kitchen is a mess, and you just wish the kids could put themselves to bed. That is also when you notice the baby is making eye contact with you for the first time or when your child says "I love you." I have said, "You read the story tonight. I am too tired." Then little fingers turn the pages. The roles are reversed. The blanket gently is tucked in around you, the parent. You are the center of each other's Universe.

A nightly family ritual might look like this:

- dinner
- pick up toys
- bath time
- pajamas
- time to use the toilet or change the diaper
- brush teeth
- read 2 books
- tucked in
- Kisses and good night

Sometimes, there are nightly prayers, a lullaby, and giving thanks. Pick two things you are grateful for in your day. Then it is the child's turn. Before they are old enough to do this, you can do it for them. "I bet you are grateful for Mommy taking you outside today. I bet you are grateful for all the stories we read."

Another ritual is naming all the people who love your child. Or naming the people, places and things you each love. Feelings of belonging and security will be abundant.

Babies learn to sleep through the night with nighttime rituals. Their bodies are tuned in from the repetition of the rituals of bedtime and their natural sleep pattern takes over. This does not mean there are not sleepless nights, bad dreams, tummy aches and all the other experiences associated with early childhood. One way to set a positive, loving environment for sleep is through the practice of a nightly ritual. Many adults, also read before closing their eyes for the night. If a child still has difficulty falling asleep after listening to a story, provide a night light with a timer and some books to look at on their own.

The night is over and a new day has begun. Your child hands you a book. Do you read it ? Of course. Reading can happen at any time. My older daughter has always brought books for her children no matter where they go. Now as a pre-teen and teenager they always have a book with them. Their books lay on the back seat of the car, under the front seat, on the floor and of course there is one in their hands. When they were little, an ottoman with a lid for storage held many books. Their neatly stored books were spread all about during the day.

Waiting is hard for children. Bring some books to the **doctor's office**. One day my younger daughter and I had a long wait at the pediatrician's office. She did not want to be there in the first place. Totally and completely frustrated, she stood up, called me by my first name loud enough for everyone to hear, and declared, "Susan, I am leaving." Years later, it is funny, not so much as it was happening. I should have packed some books.

Bring books to the **dentist office** and the **hair salon**.

Have you ever heard "How much longer?" over and over again from the back seat? You want to pull your hair out! Bring books on every **car trip**. Include audio books and coloring books, and books on CD that you all enjoy. Going on a **jet**? Bring some books. The other passengers may be glad you did.

Read outside at the **pool**. The children, tired from all the activity, warming themselves in an over-sized towel stretched out on a chaise, in the shade or in the sun, may welcome an adventure, or something to stir their imagination. Maybe they would enjoy some poetry written by Shel Silverstein. What a perfect time and place for reading! At a public pool you may find there are lots of little ones interested in listening to the story.

Put a blanket **on the grass** in the park and read aloud while also hearing the birds sing and feeling the breeze on your skin. Find a bench or sit **under a big oak tree** and read out loud.

After roasting marshmallows and listening to the crackling of the **campfire**, the mood is perfect for a story.

Sitting on the porch, at the beach, in a tent, at a **picnic table**, on **a blanket on the grass** in the morning, afternoon or night, which is your favorite?

The message here is a bedtime ritual of reading provides a warm, soothing, safe, cozy experience.

Daytime reading can be silly, loud, raucous, exciting and delicious. Then at nap time, tone it down again.

This is not school, there are no quizzes. Make sure you are both enjoying the experience.

More places to read to your child:

- On a bus, a plane, a train or bus
- At the library
- At a bookstore
- In front of a fireplace
- On the floor
- In a tree
- Under a homemade fort
- On a swing
- Under the covers
- On a window seat
- On your lap

Show Up
Take Action

The fact that you are this far along reading this book says you are already showing up for your child and taking action. Congratulations. Both reading books and interacting with books are part of the recipe for your child's success. To make this work you need books. Books can be found at obvious places like libraries, so if you do not have one, get a library card. As I stated previously, children are eligible for library cards at birth.

Children's books are available for purchase at your local bookstores, Barnes and Noble, Target, Walmart, Amazon, and sometimes at the drug store and grocery store.

Discount books can be found at Goodwill and online at, kidsbooks.com , an online outlet for children's books. These books are from excess inventory from publishers.

Look for books at yard sales, book fairs, and at Little Free Libraries, the boxes you see near the sidewalk in many neighborhoods. Anyone can take a book or share a book. Enter your zip code at littlefreelibrary.org to find a nearby location.

Unite for Literacy (uniteforliteracy.com) provides free access to hundreds of digital picture books. The illustrations are bright and inviting. Many of the books are translated in over 30 different languages including Chinese, French, American Sign Language, and Arabic.

An extraordinary gift to literacy is Dolly Parton's Imagination Library (imaginationlibrary.com). Each month, your child aged birth to five years of age, will receive an age-appropriate book at no cost. Dolly, an exceptional human being, wants children to be excited about books and the magic they bring to their lives regardless of their family's worth.

Scholastic (shop.scholastic.com) is a popular site for purchasing new books that your kids will love. My colleagues and I often found our student's favorite books from Scholastic. Scholastic offers a Facebook page for parents.

Some school districts are now preventing teachers from purchasing books for use in their classrooms, but as parents you can give your child access to the magic of reading without censorship. Books are not diseases. Read each book first. You decide, not someone who probably did not even read the book they are trying to keep you from reading. Some books are banned because they include the word "magic". What would Disney World be without the Magic Kingdom, a place to dream, imagine and wish upon a star?

This is your life, your journey. This is your child's life and your family's life and journey. Make it limitless. Make it joyful. The power is yours.

How to Interact with a Book

Get cozy and be yourself.

Reading is good, reading and interacting is even better, reading, interacting and enjoying the experience is the best.

Here are suggestions on how to interact:

You and your little one are looking at the cover and pointing to things you notice. You read, out loud, the title, the author's name and the illustrator's name.

You read the story.

After repeated readings of one of their favorite books, make a mistake. Did your child notice? If not, keep reading the same book. If they do notice, then say oops, how does that part go? Doing this lets you know how well your child knows the story.

Be expressive, pause, whisper, use a high voice and a low voice, play the character, or be soothing and calm. Read the room. You will know what is right for the given situation.

This is not the time for a speedy bullet train. It is good to view the scenery along the way. In other words, read slower than you are used to. Little ears take time to process what they are listening to. The sounds of speech, the rhyming, the flow, the word order, and the thoughts require mental maps and internal navigation. Your child is building his memory and attention. Your child is learning to listen and is hearing lots of new words. It is not just the number of words but the variety as well. The language of books is different from the language of conversations.

Reading the story the same way every time makes it predictable and easier for the child to "read" themselves. Although, they are not technically reading, kids will turn the pages eventually and tell you the story.

When you are reading to your baby, they are learning about numbers, letters, colors, shapes and body parts. It is a lot to learn. It is also so much fun to play Peek-a-boo and How Big is Baby? while you gently stretch their arms up. Birth to age five is like no other time for brain development and learning. It is spectacular. And by reading aloud to your child you are having a massive positive influence.

Look for a letter, not any letter. Look for the first letter of your child's name. Point to it. Look on every page. Now try M for Mommy or D for Daddy. Get the refrigerator magnet letters and use those.

Find words repeated in stories. Point to them. Not just nouns. Look for 'the", "and", "because".

Sing along with Old MacDonald, jump like the Five Little Monkeys jumping on the bed.

Talk about Clifford the big, red dog. What are the parts of his body? Paws, a tail, fur. You are guiding your child to understand the concept of parts and whole.

When re-reading Brown Bear, Brown Bear What Do You See? Change it to your child's name or Grandpa, Grandpa what do you see? Daddy, Daddy, Mommy, Mommy, a sister's name or a brother's name. Make it silly, make it fun.

Go to the zoo and see a real bear. Has anyone in your family ever seen a bear at Yellowstone or in the wild? What happened? Ask them to predict what happened.

Read the story and let the children fill in the blank. Brown Bear Brown Bear what do you _____?

Ask how a story makes them feel.

Ask your child if they like the story and why but do not make it a quiz. This is interacting not teaching with quizzes and exams.

Read Frog and Toad or Winnie the Pooh, or any book with multiple characters. Which character do they like best? Why?

Discuss how the characters in a story help each other. How do you help other members in your family?

If you work out of town, Zoom or FaceTime to read a story. Do not forget to pack a few books before you leave. This is a great way for family members who live far away to have story time with the child as well.

Tell stories of your childhood.

Make up your own stories. Once upon a time, there was a little girl named Mia. She had pretty brown eyes and a cute little nose. It can be real or silly.

When I held babies in the NICU, I would tell them stories: Once upon a time there was a baby named Izzy. She was born in Austin, Texas. She was so tiny. She was born too early and she needed to stay in a very special little crib that could keep her warm and keep out germs.

Take photos on your phone, then with your child, give them captions. You have made a photo storybook of your own. Print it out at Walgreen's, Shutterfly or any site you choose.

Take photos of silly things your dog does and make it into a book.

Read the "Pigeon" books by Mo Willems and have a "Pigeon Party." Serve hot dogs.

Have a "Little Red Hen" picnic and bring bread.

Invite your child's favorite stuffed animals, trucks or Legos to listen to a story.

There are countless ways to make reading aloud fun, but if the child is not enjoying the experience, just stop and do it another time.

Reading aloud is a spectacular vehicle for getting to know each other. What is your purpose? Yes, you want to do the number one best thing to help with their future success. You also want to have happy, healthy children who feel loved, who feel safe, who know the importance of having gratitude and compassion.

This is not a race. It is not to see who can read the most books. It is not to compare yourself or your child to anyone else. This is more like Friday night pizza and Sunday pancakes. A relaxed, time away from phones and TVs. It is a flight on a magic carpet, it is a discussion. (Could the wolf have eaten salad instead of grandma or the little pigs?) It may become the best part of your day and your child's.

The Little Red Hen
Paul Galdone

Interactive Ideas.

Here are some ideas on how to interact with this book with your child.

From the cover

- Can you find a hoe? A vine? A rake? A caterpillar? A sun?

- What do you think this story will be about?

From the title page.

- Point to the clothesline and say this is a clothesline for drying clothes outside.

- Point to the bird house and say this is a birdhouse.

- Point to the caterpillar and say this is a caterpillar.

- Point to the clothes pins and say these are clothespins to keep the clothes from falling off the line.

- Let's find the mailboxes. Who has the largest one? Who has the smallest one? What kind of mail do you think they would get? A birthday invitation?

- Do you see the smoke stack? How about the sunflowers?

- What is the cat dreaming of on the soft, red couch? (Sardines)

- What is the dog dreaming of while sleeping on the hammock? (Dog bone)

- What is the mouse dreaming of? (Swiss cheese)

- What is in the mouse's room?

What does the Hen use to make bread?

Milk, Sugar, Eggs, Butter, Fine white flour

Rhyming words

Wheat, beat, heat, meat, neat

The Three Billy Goats Gruff Little Golden Book

I suggest reading this fairy tale from Norway and interacting after reading the story. Read it again and again. Pick one of these activities at a time. Role play being the troll or a Billy goat. Make it fun. These ideas are just activities to help you get started. Do what is joyful for you and your child.

<u>GOAT begins with </u> G goat, grass, green get, go, going, gobble

<u>Rhyming words</u>

Goat, boat, float, coat, throat

Goat Facts

1. Billy Goats are boys.

2. Nanny goats are girls.

3. A baby goat is called a kid.

4. A baby goat's birth is called kidding.

5. Baby goats weigh between four to twelve pounds at birth.

6. Baby goats can stand and walk right after birth.

The Three Billy Goats cross the bridge to eat the sweet, green grass.

I would cross the bridge to eat hot popcorn.

I would cross the bridge to eat a cold, ice cream cone.

I would cross the bridge to eat a juicy slice of watermelon.

I would cross the bridge to eat _____.

Big Billy Goat Gruff is the oldest. Who is the oldest in our family? Who is the youngest.

Extension: Build a bridge (use pillows, Legos, paper, get creative).

Don't Let the Pigeon Drive the Bus

Mo Willems

Read the title and author's name. You will be reading this book many times. The questions are not meant to quiz your child. The questions are a way for you to interact with both the story and with each other. The "P" words and the rhyming words help with speech development and pre-reading skills development.

Pigeon begins with "P" please, pig, play, pull, pizza, pet, party, potato, pink, park

Rhyming words

Let, vet, bet, yet, get, jet, wet

Discussion

- Ask your child questions.
- The Pigeon really wants to drive the bus. Should we let him?
- Why not?
- The Pigeon says," I never get to do anything!". Do you ever feel that way?
- How do you feel when we say NO when you want to do something?
- Why do you think we say NO sometimes?
- What are some things you want to do but you think we will say No?
- What animal do you think would make a great driver?
- Would you like to drive a bus?
- Would you rather have a pet pigeon or a pet dinosaur?

Just for fun

- Do pigeons really talk?
- How do you know a pigeon is a bird?
- If you could be an animal, what animal would you choose?
- Do you like the Pigeon? Why?
- If you had a pet pigeon, what would you name it?

I Was So Mad
Mercer Mayer

<u>Rhyming Words</u> - mad, sad, bad, Dad, glad <u>Activities</u>

- Role play examples: Reverse roles. Parents asks child, "I want to jump on the bed." Child says, "No." Parent says, "I am so mad." Parent says, "I want candy for dinner." Child says, "No." Parent says, "I am so mad." This is meant to be done in a humorous was to incite giggles. Use your own made-up scenarios to enjoy.

Count the frogs in the bathroom.

Find the words no, Mom, Dad, and mad in the story.

<u>Conversation starters</u>

- Do you ever feel mad like the Little Critter? When?

- What do you do to stop feeling mad?

- How old do you think Little Critter is?

- Little Critter packed chocolate chip cookies. What is your favorite kind of cookie?

- How does Little Critter feel on the last page at the end of the story? Why?

- What season is it in this story? How do you know?

- Did you like this story? Do you think someone else would like it?

The Neonatal Intensive Care Unit

"Sometimes, the smallest things take up the most room in your heart."
Unknown

An estimated 10% to 15% of newborns will spend time in the NICU.

When your child arrives early and cannot go home with you, or arrives with health issues, the NICU, Neonatal Intensive Care Unit, has specially trained, nurses, doctors, feeding specialists, and many others there to give their attention to your baby's well-being.

First there is the Neonatologist, a physician who specializes in newborn care. Other doctors who attend to babies in the NICU include cardiologists, neurologists, ophthalmologists and surgeons. Other professional staff include physical therapists, occupational therapists, speech language pathologists, social workers, and pastoral care workers.

Your infant may be assigned to an isolette or open crib. Monitors to measure heart rate, breathing and blood oxygen levels surround each crib or incubator. To help with breathing, there are ventilators or a plastic tube inserted at the nose called a cannula.

So, why is this included in a guide on reading aloud to your child? It is simple. It is never too early to introduce books to your child! If your baby is in the NICU, then that is a good place to start.

I have observed parents in the NICU reading to their babies. As a volunteer in the NICU, I read books to babies. At first, though, I wondered why there were books in the NICU. It seemed an unusual place for books. The babies need to rest. I learned the babies also need soft voices calming them. According to Georgetown University researchers, reading aloud to babies can cause both the heartbeat and breathing to become more stable.

It is never too early to introduce books to your child.

At Sharp Mary Birch Hospital for Women and Newborns, a program called PRiNT, Parent Reading in

NICU Therapy, was initiated by nurses Elsa Stout and Rachelle Sey. The parents were given a bag full of books with an image of baby foot prints and the words "NICU where little things matter." Stout believed reading to the infants would bring healing to both parents and child, decrease stress and increase bonding.

Parents are crucial to their baby's development. Holding their baby's hand or cuddling their baby or providing skin-to skin contact (kangarooing) provides the human touch of healing. Softly speaking, singing and reading are also important for calming the baby and bonding with the baby.

While you may be worrying about weight gain and a healthy heart rate, reading gives you something to do which is natural and requires no special equipment. Reading aloud is a normal activity. The equipment and professionals do what they need to do. Parents give powerful doses of love and healing by cuddling, singing, talking, and reading.

For the times you cannot be there, you can record your voice on a device and the nurses will play that for your baby. You can record singing some lullabies and of course, you can read to them. Pandora has lullabies you can play on your phone while holding your baby.

Remember, you are contributing to your baby's brain development, health and growth with your soothing voice, gentle touch and loving heart. It may not be measurable by some machine, yet it is powerful, beautiful and healing. You bring a sense of security. You are already laying the foundation for your child's future success.

Not all Kids are the Same

"That's the thing about books.
They let you travel without
moving your feet."
Jhumpa Lahiri

One of my favorite students was a boy named Jerry. His previous therapist was gifted. It was as if she was born to work with students like Jerry. So when she retired, the team discussed the change in our caseloads and Jerry, who was a teenager by this time, became my student.

Jerry was always accompanied by a full-time nurse, his mother or both. Jerry did not walk, talk or eat.

He could not swallow. His nutritional needs arrived through a tube.

He had severe scoliosis, puffy little hands and feet, skinny legs. It may not sound like it, but Jerry was handsome. He did not breathe unassisted, yet somehow, he could set the alarm off on the machine keeping him alive. This most often occurred during school assemblies. His mouth stayed permanently open. Most of the day, he sat in a large wheelchair, and part of everyday, he needed to be lifted out of his wheelchair. He had minimal control of his eyes, thumbs and knees, so those body parts were what we could work with in therapy. He could also vocalize loudly! And although I was his speech therapist, he never spoke a word.

None of this really describes Jerry because despite his body there was a really cool boy inside. He knew how to make a friend. He knew how to survive and I really think he enjoyed so much about his life. I read books to him. What was even more fun, though was the books we created together.

Jerry's nurse and Mom took photos of Jerry's experiences. We uploaded the photos to the computer and put them in a sequence to tell a story. It was basically a slide show. The story was told through the photo captions. Jerry used his thumb to activate a small switch, and like turning a page, the next photo would appear on the screen. He could then return to his classroom with a way to communicate his story to his classmates.

There is an important reason Jerry's story is included in a book about reading aloud to babies through five-year old's. If his mother had left him in a corner while she busied herself with the other children or did not introduce him to books and experiences like all the other children, he would not have had the comprehension and understanding he had when I was his therapist. He may have been trapped in a body with severe medical issues, yet he learned, participated and was part of a school, part of a community and part of a family.

Children with special needs are still children! Did you notice I did not use Jerry's diagnosis? That is because a diagnosis is helpful but it does not define anyone. I can say with 100% certainty that reading aloud to children, talking to them about what you are reading and interacting with them is one of the most important, powerful actions that parents can do daily. It is the daily commitment that will have enormous payoffs.

Reading aloud to children is a normal activity. It says I see you as a human being, I have hope for your future and I am going to feed your brain, soothe you with my voice, and love you dearly.

If your little one cannot easily move their hands to point to a picture in the baby board book you are reading and exploring, gently guide their hand. Hand over hand is a beginning. Hold their hand and point together.

If their eye gaze is still developing, move the book around to where it is most comfortable for their viewing. Be patient, let their eyes find what it is you are looking at, and praise them for their interactions.

If your child cannot get up and select a book, maybe they can choose it in a different way. The adult holds up two books, and the child can select the book based on the one they are looking at, pointing to, a thumbs up or vocalizing.

We all understand words long before we can say them. Babies are not born talking. They listen and learn speech as we talk to them and read to them. The language of books is more complex than the language of conversation.

If your child is not talking, it does not mean they are not listening. I had a student who attended my school just for summer school, so I did not know him well. All summer, he barely spoke to me, that is until the last day. During our sessions, we had listened to environmental sounds like waves, a fire engine siren and so forth. He could point to the photos of the beach or the fire truck. If he did not say the word, I would provide it for him.

After a while, if I said beach, he said the shore. If I said merry-go-round, he said carousel. He knew more than I was giving him credit for. On the last day, he told me in complete sentences what he thought of our summer together. This boy who did not talk to me for six weeks said, "Mrs. Jarvis, I really enjoyed our summer together. Thank you."

Not only was he listening, he demonstrated that he had already learned a higher level of vocabulary. He was diagnosed as being Autistic. His Mom was a special education teacher. If we had more time together I would have certainly stepped up my game. I underestimated him, and yet, he was patient with me. We don't often use words like carousel in our conversations. I believe this boy learned a great deal from being read to by his mom.

There is a lot we cannot control as parents. There is a lot we worry about, too. Your child is deaf, or blind, has cerebral palsy or motor function disorder, or you fear they will stop breathing. In truth the list is very long. There are over six billion kids in American schools getting services for disabilities. Reading to your child every day is something you can control and do every day. It is even more important for kids with challenges.

As a teenage mom, I had no concept of the importance of reading aloud to my baby. Some experts suggest if a child without special circumstances is read the same book one hundred times the child with special circumstances may need the same book five hundred times. Each time the book is read the child gets a little more out of the experience. Have you ever watched a movie for a second or third time and wondered how did I miss that? Or, have you re-read a book and discovered more through the second reading? You know your child. Everyone is different. You have control. Just read!

It is never too early to start reading to your child, it is also never too late. The most benefits occur as the child's brain is developing between birth and age five but that does not mean give up after age five. The amount of exposure children have to the language of books is tremendous and brings them greater success in school and in life.

Sometimes parents of children with special needs feel ashamed, not good enough, isolated or damaged. Guess what? You can change those thoughts. You are valued. Life is a journey not a competition. Ask for help if you can. I am writing this section so you will feel included on this path. I am not leaving your children behind. I want you to feel empowered.

I made so many mistakes as a parent. But now I get to watch my daughter be a parent and I am in awe. She seems to know just how to make her children feel loved and cared for, important, and treasured. I love how her children are readers and ask permission to buy books from their local bookstore.

One step at a time. Start today. If your child cannot sit for a book and is rolling on the floor, read it anyway. If your child is in the hospital, read to him or her. Make it fun and joyful.

Adaptive Equipment

If your child has Cerebral Palsy, the most common motor disability in children, or another condition that makes turning the page challenging, Special Educators and Occupational Therapists have found many creative ways that give children access to common activities.

Binder clips, paper clips, removable puffy balls, hand splints and page turners attached to headgear are some of the possible solutions. Ask for help from an expert in assistive technology and adaptive equipment for children.

Non-verbal children can interact with the use of switches also called buttons, BigMacks, and Jelly Beans. The switches/buttons are small, lightweight, battery powered and fairly indestructible. These switches can be ordered through Amazon and other companies online. They can be recorded to say, "Turn the page."

They can be recorded to repeat the rhyme in a story "Brown Bear Brown Bear what do you see?" They can be recorded with anything you choose so the child will enjoy reading and feel part of the experience.

Technology changes rapidly so my advice is to consult an expert as needed and remember reading to all children is important and necessary for their development.

Affirmations

"Every storm eventually
runs out of rain."
Maya Angelou

One of my goals in writing this book is to empower, you, the reader, to take action by making a commitment to read, talk, and listen to your children daily and build a future of success. You will be far more likely to read, to engage with your child, and have fun in the process if you feel confident, resilient and aligned with your core values.

Parenthood is probably the most challenging task you could undertake. You have probably heard the phrase "It takes a village to raise a child." No one does it alone. Grandparents, cousins, aunts and uncles, neighbors, teachers, coaches, and friends all play a role.

In my case, a fellow student came to my rescue. I was a teenage mom with a husband struggling to support us. I was attending college as a day student when the babysitter canceled on the day of an important exam. I put my baby in her car seat and drove the thirty minutes to the campus. I was late. The professor saw me with my child and told me she could not help me. I would get an F for not taking the exam. The classroom door was open, the other students could hear what was happening. A fellow student came out and told me she would finish her exam quickly and then watch my daughter, so I could take the exam.

Unbelievable right? I could not do it alone. The world is benevolent. Things always work out for me. Things always work out.

It wasn't until later, when I was a mother of three, divorced, remarried and facing many internal struggles, that I learned of affirmations. I hated myself. I felt like a failure. A therapist told me to repeat these words all day if I needed to, "I walk in strength and beauty." I did what she said. I held my head up and inside I repeated, "I walk in strength and beauty. *I* walk in strength and beauty. I walk in *strength* and beauty. I walk in strength and *beauty.*" In other words I am valuable, intelligent, strong and I am a good person.

So when you are too tired, your child is the only child in the pre-school who is napping alone, outside the room, your dog has just vomited all over, and the world is coming down on you, pick an affirmation.

Affirmations are also called power statements. Power statements empower your life. We all get triggered by doubts, fatigue, and limiting beliefs. These power statements or affirmations support you in changing your mindset. It does not matter whether you call them affirmations or power statements. What does matter is that you use something that is right for you.

In the beginning, when you use your power statement, it may feel like you are just repeating a bunch or words. Then, gradually, you will say it, and feel it in your bones and heart. Isn't that what Nike was counting on with their slogan, "Just Do IT". Mind shift.

I have listed several affirmations. I use them because they work. Write your own. Teach them to your children.

You already have a vision of what you want. You want to raise your child to feel loved, cared for and safe. You want your child to develop speech and language skills and an abundance of wonderful vocabulary words. You want your child to learn how to be social, make friends and have empathy. You want your child to be able to focus and concentrate. You want your child to laugh, giggle, and play. You want your child to use their imagination. You want your child to succeed in school, and most of all, you want your child to succeed in life.

These power statements are merely a tool to support you on this journey of reading and parenting. Your state of mind and confidence are vitally important. Repeating positive statements to yourself builds your confidence thereby making taking action easier as well.

I am equipped to handle every situation I encounter.

I am confident.

I find joy in my children.

I am a positive role model for my children.

I am strong and resilient.

Things happen for me, not to me.

I choose to be happy.

I am here to learn, not to be perfect.

I will not compare myself or my child to others.

Today, I will laugh.

I listen to my intuition.

Difficult is not impossible.

One day at a time.

I choose to feel calm.

Things always work out.

I can keep going even when things are tough.

I do not take anything personally.

I release the past and embrace the present.

I am patient.

I accept and love myself completely.

Each day I do the best I can.

It is okay to ask for help.

I am a person of value.

I have been through much worse.

Nothing can stop me.

I choose hope over fear.

I believe in me (to yourself).

I believe in you (to your child).

I am full of love, full of life, and full of hope.

Frequently Asked Questions

<u>When should I start reading to my child?</u>

There is no such thing as starting too early. Parents talk to and read to their pregnant belly. Parents in the NICU read to their babies. My infant daughter's Dad read her the newspaper or the magazine article he was reading. He also introduced her to the library. She ended up with a perfect score on the verbal section of her SAT.

<u>How often should I read the same book?</u>

Children will ask for the same book over and over until they find something they like more. You can read a book one hundred times and that is okay. Research has shown that children with learning difficulties might need the same book read three to five times more than other children. Read more than one book not just the favorite.

<u>Should I quiz my child about the books we read?</u>

No. Ask questions, ask opinions, and make this experience loving and fun for both of you and the whole family.

<u>My toddler cannot sit still for story time. What should I do?</u>

Do not give up and do not force it. Perhaps, read a story during bath time, involve toys or stuffed animals, or put on a story while going for a car ride. Read a story while pushing a stroller at the zoo, or read to one of your other children while the toddler is in the room. You could pair cookies and milk with story time. Make up your own story. For example, Sydney and Mommy went to the grocery store today and what did they see?

Read your recipe while cooking dinner. Read the street signs. Just be creative and let it flow.

<u>My child has physical disabilities. How do I know if reading is beneficial?</u>

Maybe your child will not be able to demonstrate right now that they are developing and growing through this experience. Teachers are able to identify the children who have heard stories, who have had lots of parental attention, who understand directions, and who are more aware of a world around them.

One of my favorite students could not speak, walk or breathe on his own. But guess what? He enjoyed books. We even created our own books that he shared with his classmates.

Reading is valuable and you reading to your child, bonding and connecting with love and joy is the most valuable gift.

<u>My child does not look at me or the book. Should I still keep reading?</u>

Yes, keep reading but try a variety of books, simpler, harder, non-fiction. Talk about the book to someone else and notice if your child is listening. While eye contact is valuable it does not always mean someone is not listening. Children with neurodiverse behaviors may not use eye contact. Keep reading.

What Not to Do

> "Reading aloud should not be presented to children as a chore or duty. It should be offered to them as a precious gift."
> *Kate DiCamillo*

1. Do not make reading aloud time "school time".

This is not a guide for teachers. This is a guide for parents, family and caregivers. Reading aloud as presented here is not for the purpose of formal teaching. It should be natural and FUN. This is playing and fairy tales, pirates, and dinosaurs. It is space rockets and magic carpet rides.

2. No quizzing.

Quizzing implies there are right and wrong answers. Ask for opinions instead.

3. No tests.

Testing also implies right and wrong answers and perhaps repeating the correct answer, writing answers, and an assessment versus a discussion. Looking at the cover of a book and asking if the child has an idea what the story may be about the first time is exploring. Repeating this every time the book is read is monotonous.

4. No punishment or threats.

For example, if you do not put your toys away there will be no story tonight.

5. Do not substitute movies and books on the Internet for the experience of you reading aloud.

The experience of holding your child and reading aloud has benefits not achieved by giving a toddler an I Pad with a story.

Book List

This is Where to Start with your Baby

Pick any book on this list and have fun!!

"Whose Knees Are These?" by Jabari Asim

"But Not the Hippopotamus" by Sandra Boynton

"The Going to Bed Book" by Sandra Boynton

Goodnight Moon" by Margaret Wise Brown

"The Runaway Bunny" by Margaret Wise Brown

"One, Two, Buckle My Shoe" by Jane Cabrera

"Dear Zoo" by Rod Campbell

"Brown Bear, Brown Bear, What Do You See?" By Bill Martin, Jr. / Eric Carle

"You're Okay!" By Joy Cho

"My Dreams: Baby Basics" by Xavier Deneux

"Fuzzy Yellow Duckling" by Matthew Van Fleet

"Ten Little Fingers and Ten Little Toes" by Mem Fox

"Time for Bed" by Mem Fox

"Where is the Green Sheep?" By Mem Fox

"The Itsy Bitsy Spider" by Maddie Frost

"Bus Stops" by Taro Gomi

"Where's Spot?" by Eric Hill

"Smile" by Roberta Grobel Intrater

"Moomin's Little Book of Words" by Tove Jansson

"Where Is Baby's Belly Button?" by Karen Katz

"Pat the Bunny" by Dorothy Kunhardt

"Diggers Go" by Steve Light

"Chicka Chicka Boom Boom" by Bill Martin, Jr. and John Archambault

"Guess How Much I Love You" by Sam McBratney

"Baby Faces" by Kate Merritt

"Lots of Lambs" by Laura Numeroff

"All Fall Down" by Helen Oxenbury

"First 100 Words" by Roger Priddy

"Good Night Gorilla" by Peggy Rathmann

Dragons, Caterpillars, Frogs and Toads

"The Babies and Doggies Book" by John Schindel and Molly Woodward

"The Wheels on the Tuk Tuk" by Kabir Sehgal

"I Love You Through and Through" by Bernadette Rossetti-Shustak

"The Wheels on the Bus" by Tiger Tales

"Max's First Word" by Rosemary Wells

"Bear Snores On" by Karma Wilson

Okay, you are doing great! Have you reached baby's first year? Again, start anywhere, choose what you like. Read favorite books over and over. Read slowly.

"Duck in the Truck" by Jez Alborough

"Hug" by Jez Alborough

"Who Sank the Boat?" By Pamela Allen

"Dinosaur Dance" by Sandra Boynton

"Clifford the Big Red Dog" Norman Bridwell

"Stomp,Wiggle, Clap and Tap" by Rachelle Burk

"The Very Hungry Caterpillar" by Eric Carle

"The Happy Lion" by Louise Fatio

"Bark George" by Jules Feiffer

"Quantum Physics for Babies" by Chris Ferrie

"Corduroy" by Dan Freeman

"Global Babies" by The Global Fund for Children

"I Hear a Pickle" by Rachel Isadora

"The Snowy Day" by Ezra Jack Keats

"Never Feed a Yeti Spaghetti" by Make Believe Ideas Ltd.

"I was So Mad" by Mercer Mayer

"When We Were Very Young" by A.A. Milne"

Dragons, Caterpillars, Frogs and Toads

"Utterly Lovely One" by Mary Murphy

The Littlest Dragon by Susan Quinn

"Solomon Crocodile" by Catherine Rayner

"Lots of Feelings" by Shelley Rotner

"Little Blue Truck" by Alice Schertle and Jill McElmurry

"The Napping House" by Audrey Wood

Dr. Seuss

D r. Seuss, an award-winning author, wrote over 60 books. Children adore these books. I suggest starting with the titles listed below.

"The Cat in the Hat"

"The Cat in the Hat Comes Back"

"Dr. Seuss's ABC"

"Fox in Socks"

"Green Eggs and Ham"

"Hop on Pop"

"Horton Hears a Who"

"The Lorax"

"One Fish, Two Fish, Red Fish, Blue Fish"

"Oh the Places You'll Go!"

Mo Willems

❦

Mo Willems is a NYTimes bestselling author and illustrator. My students loved the Pigeon Series, and I loved reading these stories too.

"Knuffle Bunny: A Cautionary Tale"

"Knuffle Bunny Too"

"Knuffle Bunny Free: An Unexpected Diversion"

"Don't Let the Pigeon Stay Up"

"Don't Let the Pigeon Drive the Bus!"

"The Pigeon Finds a Hot Dog"

"The Pigeon Wants a Puppy"

"The Pigeon HAS to go to School"

"The Pigeon will Ride the Roller Coaster"

"The Pigeon Needs a Bath"

"Waiting is Not Easy"

"We Are in a Book!"

What are your child's favorite books so far? Keep reading the favorites. Here are more books. By now you have moved beyond board books. The stories are longer, and you are enriching your child's world, building their vocabulary and memory while enjoying the most beautiful bonds of child and parent.

"The Jolly Postman" by Janet and Alan Ahlberg

"Miss Nelson is Missing" by Harry Allard

"Cloudy with a Chance of Meatballs" by Judy Barrett

"Madeline" by Ludwig Bemelmans

"Z is for Moose" by Kelly Bingham

"The Mitten" by Jan Brett

"Arthur" by Marc Brown

"Mike Mulligan and his Steam Shovel" by Virginia Lee Burton

"The Thank You Letter" by Jane Cabrera

"But Excuse Me That is My Book" by Lauren Child

"I am Absolutely Too Small for School" by Lauren Child

"Misty the Cloud: Friends Through Rain or Shine" by Dylan Dreyer and Rosie Butcher

"Misty the Cloud: A Very Stormy Day" by Dylan Dreyer and Rosie Butcher

"Possum Magic" by Mem Fox

"Danny and the Dinosaur" by Syd Hoff

"The Gingerbread Man" by Eric Kimmel

"I Want My Hat Back" by Jon Klassen

"The Story of Ferdinand" by Munro Leaf

"Frog and Toad are Friends" by Arnold Lobel

"That's What Leprechaun's Do" by Emily Arnold McCully

"I Need a New Butt" by Dawn McMillan

"What if You Could Sniff Like a Shark?: Explore the Superpowers of Ocean

Animals" by Sandra Markle and Howard McWilliam

"What if You Had T. Rex Teeth?: And Other Dinosaur Parts" by Sandra Markle and Howard McWilliam

"Winnie-the-Pooh" by A.A. Milne

"If You Give a Mouse A Cookie" by Laura Numeroff

"If You Give a Moose A Muffin" by Laura Numeroff

"Fancy Nancy" by Jane O'Connor

"The Little Red Hen" by Jerry Pinkney

"The Little Engine that Could" by Watty Piper

"The Tale of Peter Rabbit" by Beatrix Potter

"Curious George" by H. A. Rey

"The Word Collector" by Peter H. Reynolds

"We are Going on a Bear Hunt" by Michael Rosen

"I Got the Rhythm" by Connie Schofield-Morrison

"Where the Wild Things Are" by Maurice Sendak

"Sheep in a Jeep" by Nancy Shaw

"Where the Sidewalk Ends" by Shel Siverstein

"The Wonkey Donkey" by Craig Smith

"Minerva Louise" by Janet Morgan Stoeke

"Namaste is a Greeting" by Suma Subrahamiam

"There Was an Old Woman Who Swallowed A Fly" by Simms Taback

"Eloise" by Kay Thompson

"Eloise in Paris" by Kay Thompson

"Anatole" by Eve Titus

"Press Here" by Henre Tullet

"Lyle, Lyle Crocodile" by Bernard Waber

"A Chair for My Mother" by Vera Williams

"In My Heart" Jo Witek

"Alexander and the Terrible, Horrible, No Good, Very Bad Day" by Judith Viorst

"I Got the Rhythm" by Connie Schofield-Morrison

Robert Munsch

❦

Best-selling author, Robert Munsch, knows children. He worked in daycare centers and nursery schools while earning his degree in Early Childhood Education.

I read his books to my speech therapy students. One day, my student, Jessica, a beautiful six-year old with long, straight, messy dark-blonde hair was escorted to my classroom by her teacher. Jessica was born with Fetal Alcohol Syndrome and the firm grasp her teacher had on her hand, told me Jessica was having one her "active" days. I usually picked her up from her classroom.

Jessica kicked off her shoes and sat at my table. "I found my father," she told me. "He was on the porch. He wrote my name." The note on his chest said, "I love you, Jessica."

Next, she crawled into my lap and asked for her favorite book, I'll Love You Forever by Robert Munsch.

We rocked back and forth as I read the refrain: "I'll love you forever, I'll like you for always as long as I am living, my baby you will be."

I did not know any details, but my intuition told me something important had happened in Jessica's life. A few days later, Jessica's teacher told me Jessica's father committed suicide, and Jessica was the first person to find him when she came home from school.

A week later, a High School Counselor arrived at our school to see Jessica. He told me he helped high school students with their post high school plans, not six year old's dealing with trauma. He told me, he was not prepared for this. I told him to read her favorite story and do not be surprised if she crawls up on your lap.

He needed to use my speech therapy room, so I left "I'll Love You Forever" on the table. I knew what Jessica needed. When they were together she did not want to talk, she wanted to be read to and that is just what happened.

The power of a book to soothe a grieving child was unexpected and beautiful.

Robert Munsch books to enjoy include:

"Andrew's Loose Tooth"

"I'll Love You Forever"

"Paperbag Princess"

"The Sand Castle Contest"

"Show and Tell"

"Something Good

Stan and Jan Berenstain

⋆

This husband and wife team published over 200 books. This is a list of some favorites from my students. They are rich in vocabulary and fun to read. Their older books seem to be most popular and timeless.

"The Berenstain Bears and The Big Honey Hunt"

"The Berenstain Bears and the New Baby"

"The Berenstain Bears and the Sitter"

The Berenstain Bears Go to Camp"

"The Berenstain Bears In the Dark"

"The Berenstain Bears Trick or Treat"

"The Berenstain Bears Visit the Dentist"

"The Berenstain Bears We Love Baseball"

Is your child in pre-school? Approaching kindergarten? Then you have been on an amazing journey!

By reading so many books you have exposed your child to the sights and sounds of a farm, a zoo, a forest, and the beach. You have read about cars, trucks, school buses, jeeps and a tuk tuk. Things were up, down, in, out, under, over, between, near, far and beyond. You read about colors, numbers, letters, and body parts.

Maybe you laughed and maybe you cried. Maybe you all felt sleepy or felt like running around.

Keep having fun. Read some more!!!

Have some cookies and milk. Snuggle in a chair or lay on a rug. Keep reading aloud. The five year old becomes six, then seven and you may find you are still reading aloud. A father of a twelve year old boy recently told me his son loves to read. However, the Dad still reads aloud to his son because it is enjoyable to both of them.

Resources

❦

Books:

Reading Magic

Why Reading Aloud to Our Children will Change Their Lives Forever

By Mem Fox

The Enchanted Hour , The Miraculous Power of Reading Aloud in the Age of Distraction

By Meghan Cox Gurdon

The Reading Bug and How to Help Your Child Catch it

By Paul Jennings

Where to get Free books:

imaginationlibrary.com

Dolly Parton's Imagination Library will send a book, free of charge, once a month, to your child age birth to 5 years of age. Dolly Parton's Imagination Library is "dedicated to inspiring a love of reading."

littlefreelibrary.com

This non-profit organization's mission is to "build community, inspire readers and expand book access." Take a book and share a book.

It is a free book-sharing box found in many neighborhoods. You can keep the book, read it and return it, and you can donate a book.

uniteforliteracy.com

This is a digital resource offering access to beautifully illustrated books. You can listen to the books as much as you like for free. These books are

translated into many languages. An app is available as well.

storynory.com

This site provides free audio stories.

the-best-childrens-books.org

This site was created by a group of teachers to "spread the word about the very best books available for kids." This website is a resource for pre-schoolers on up. There are hundreds of book lists, helpful articles and a store to purchase new and gently used books.

More online resources

scholastic.com

Scholastic is a gold mine for parents and teachers. Read their Credo and Editorial Platform. You will find parent guides, activities, blogs and more. Join the book club, attend a book fair and purchase books at reasonable prices.

babiestobookworms.com

This is a website created by a Mom and former teacher to encourage a love of reading in children.

best-books-for-kids.com

Created by a mother of twins, this website offers information about reading books by age, book series, children's book authors and more.

kidsbook.com

This site offers a large selection of kid's books for up to 90% off the original price listed. They are new books from publishers' excess inventory.

readingrockets.org

This website is a resource for parents and teachers initiated by WETA public television. Look for their shows on PBS.

Something for parents of children with special needs

fireflyfriends.com

Check out the blog of real life stories. This website offers products to support children.

autismforlittlelearners.com

A website from a Speech Language Pathologist with lots of ideas to support parents.

A Boy Made of Blocks by Keith Stuart

A non-fiction story of a parents journey to understand his child.

Turn Autism Around: An Action Guide for Parents of Young Children with Early Signs of Autism by Mary Lynch Barbera

Certainty

❦

If you ask someone, "What are you uncertain about?" Chances are the list pops right out because it is upfront in their minds. Now I ask you. "What are you certain about?"

The pandemic had eased and I was still uncertain about going out, uncertain about getting sick, uncertain about my future. The couch became my island of security. That is until I took "one last leap of faith" and signed up for a free Tony Robbins and Dean Graziosi Master Mind course and then invested in a Master Mind Experience.

Participating in the courses and training brought me back to myself. I knew with certainty what I wanted to do. I felt an urgency. Reading, telling stories, talking about what you read are absolutely essential for navigating the world. Our children need their minds opened to a world of possibilities. They need to hear stories. I know this with certainty.

Know with certainty that you cannot fail. Know with certainty that learning and growing is about learning to be compassionate, brave, good human beings. Know with certainty that you are a powerful, loving parent offering your child a bright future. Know with complete certainty that reading aloud daily to your child is the best thing to do for your child's future because reading is an act of love.

Wishing you a wonderful, fun-filled adventure,
Susan

Acknowledgments

❦

I would like to thank all those who have guided me and assisted me including Joan Albarella, Sharon Fawley, Barbara Richardson, Matt Maier, Bridget Finn, Thomas Finn, Tracy Jarvis, Romanus Wolter, Alena Scandura, Betty Terrell, Bob Tanner, Katie Schneider, Dean Graziosi, Raf Garay, Jerry Verdi, Jessica and all my former students.

Thank you also to the divine universe that guides with love and light, energy and inspiration.

About the Author

꘎

Susan Jarvis is a retired Speech Language Pathologist, mother, grandmother and volunteer. After 30 years of developing speech, language, listening, memory and reading skills in her students, she is still passionate about empowering children and parents. She has also been a volunteer Cuddler/Rocker in the NICU in Buffalo, NY and Austin, TX, a volunteer tutor with the local literacy council, and a volunteer for a book sharing program for incarcerated individuals. She enjoys writing and her blog posts can be found at medium.com/@dunes898. She lives with her seven year old mini-Goldendoodle Abbey.

Made in the USA
Columbia, SC
15 September 2023

22869576R00052